LIFESKILLS IN ACTION

LIVING SKILLS

Cooking Your Own Meals

CARRIE
GWYNNE

LIFESKILLS IN ACTION

LIVING SKILLS

SADDLEBACK
EDUCATIONAL PUBLISHING
www.sdlback.com

All source images from Shutterstock.com

ISBN-13: 978-1-68021-043-9
ISBN-10: 1-68021-043-2
eBook: 978-1-63078-349-5

3 4873 00522 1072

Printed in Guangzhou, China
NOR/0216/CA21600250

20 19 18 17 16   1 2 3 4 5

2

Cooking.

It can seem like hard work.

There are many steps.

Plan what to eat.

Know what foods to buy.

Prepare and cook meals.

It takes time.

But making your own food is worth it.

Prepared food is made by someone else.

Buying this kind of food may be easy.

But it is not always good for us.

Most fast food is fried.

It is full of fat.

Other **ingredients** may be unhealthy too.

Frozen meals can have a lot of salt.

4

The colors or flavors may not be real.

That is why it makes sense to cook.

Buy fresh foods.

Choose spices you like.

Make healthy meals that taste great.

Buying food to make a meal may seem costly.

But think about the cost of eating out.

One time may not cost that much.

But many people eat out every day.

That adds up fast.

Cooking your own meals saves money.

How? Make one or two meals for the week.

Cook more than you need.

Put the extra food in the refrigerator.

Or freeze it.

Heat it up later that week.

Cooking does not have to take hours.

Plan ahead.

Look for an easy **recipe**.

Use a cookbook. Search online.

Then make a shopping list.

Put a few **staples** on the list.

Rice. Pasta. Potatoes. Beans.

They can be used in many meals.

You have the food.

Now get ready to cook.

Gather what you need.

Meat. Vegetables. Spices.

Trim fat from the meat.

Rinse the vegetables.

Then peel or chop them.

Measure the spices.

Choose the cooking tools.

Have them near the stove.

Basic Cookware and Tools

- One saucepan and one frying pan with lids
- Baking sheet
- Baking pan, 13" x 9"
- Chef's knife
- Paring knife
- Mixing bowl for dry ingredients
- Colander for washing vegetables and draining pasta
- Cutting board
- Measuring cups for dry ingredients
- Measuring cup for liquids
- Measuring spoons
- Tongs
- Wooden spoon
- Spatula
- Can opener
- Meat thermometer
- Towels
- Potholders

Cooking on the **stove** is easy.

But it can also be dangerous.

The burners get very hot.

Oil can splatter.

A fire can start.

Use the correct heat.

Low. Medium. High.

Watch food as it cooks.

Turn down the heat if it's too high.

Keep towels away from the stove.

Turn it off when the food is done.

The burner will be hot for a time.

Be careful not to touch it.

Preheat the oven before baking foods.

This makes it hot enough.

Food cooks all the way through.

What happens if you don't preheat?

Foods can still be **raw** inside.

Raw meat can carry germs.

Eating it can make you ill.

Most ovens have three racks.

The middle rack is used the most.

Air moves evenly around it.

Set the timer after food is in the oven.

Check once in a while.

But do not open the oven door too often.

This lets the heat out.

Food can take longer to cook.

Check the food when the timer goes off.

Make sure the food is done.

Cook it for a few more minutes if not.

An oven also has a **broiler**.

Food is placed very close to the heat.

Broiling cooks food fast.

Use a metal pan to broil.

Metal holds up in high heat.

Do not use a glass dish.

It can crack.

Watch food closely as it cooks.

A **microwave** also cooks food fast.

Use it to reheat leftovers.

Heat frozen foods here too.

It is an oven. So you can cook meals in it.

But it is not like a regular oven.

It does not heat food the same way.

The inside cooks first.

The outside does not get brown.

Food may be cold in some spots.

Find recipes in a microwave cookbook.

Start with an easy one.

Follow the safety tips.

A **crock pot** is another way to cook.

It is easy to use.

Fill it with ingredients.

Let the food cook for six to eight hours.

There is no need to stir the food.

Do other things while it cooks.

Some people even leave the house.

They come home to a hot meal.

The way food is prepared matters.

Foods can have **bacteria**.

Raw meat has juices.

The juices can get on the counter.

They can touch other foods.

Or get on your hands.

These juices can make you ill.

Fix raw meat by itself.

Be sure to wash the cutting board.

Wipe the counter too.

And wash your hands as you cook.

Keep cooked food safe.

Wrap it in foil or plastic.

Or put it in a container with a lid.

Keep the food in the refrigerator.

Or freeze it in a freezer bag.

What happens if food sits out too long?

Bacteria can grow on it.

The food can **spoil**.

You may have to throw it away.

Cooking.

It takes some time to learn.

There are steps to follow.

Start with easy recipes.

Cook one or two times a week.

Make extra food. Have leftovers.

Cooking can save time and money.

And you will know what is in your food.

Choose healthy ingredients.

Then you can feel good about what you eat.

What happens when Hunter's mom challenges him to make every family meal for the weekend? Find out in *Dinner Is Served.* Want to read on?

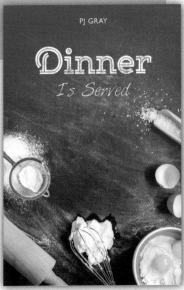

JUST *flip* THE BOOK!

Dinner

Is Served

PJ GRAY

LIFESKILLS IN ACTION

LIVING SKILLS

MONEY

Living on a Budget | Road Trip
Opening a Bank Account | The Guitar
Managing Credit | High Cost
Using Coupons | Get the Deal
Planning to Save | Something Big

LIVING

Smart Grocery Shopping | Shop Smart
Doing Household Chores | Keep It Clean
Finding a Place to Live | A Place of Our Own
Moving In | Pack Up
Cooking Your Own Meals | Dinner Is Served

JOB

Preparing a Résumé
Finding a Job
Job Interview Basics
How to Act Right on the Job
Employee Rights

SADDLEBACK
EDUCATIONAL PUBLISHING
www.sdlback.com

All source images from Shutterstock.com

ISBN-13: 978-1-68021-043-9
ISBN-10: 1-68021-043-2
eBook: 978-1-63078-349-5

Printed in Guangzhou, China
NOR/0216/CA21600250

20 19 18 17 16   1 2 3 4 5

It was Hunter's senior year. He was ready to move out. Hunter felt like an adult. He wanted to prove that he was. Hunter's mom knew how he felt. But she was not sure he was ready.

"I can take care of myself," Hunter said.

"Really?" his mom replied. "I still cook and clean for you."

"I can cook," Hunter said.

"Making a cold sandwich is not cooking."

"I can do more than that," Hunter replied.

"Want to bet?" his mom asked.

"Sure," Hunter said.

Ethan came into the room. He was Hunter's little brother.

"Okay," their mom said. "Let's make a bet. See those bags over there? I just came home from the grocery store. There is food for the whole weekend. You must cook all of our meals this weekend. Just from the food in those bags. I bet you can't."

Hunter looked at the bags.

Ethan laughed. "I bet you can't either!"

"Okay," Hunter replied. "It's a deal."

"Good," his mom said. "You must start with dinner tonight."

"But it is Friday! You said the weekend."

"Are you backing out?" she asked.

"No," Hunter said.

"Okay," his mom replied. "Good luck."

The grocery bags were on the kitchen counter. Hunter looked in each one. There were fresh vegetables. A head of lettuce. A bag of tomatoes. He found a loaf of bread. And a gallon of milk. One bag had two dozen eggs and a box of pasta. There were two cans of rolls inside too. The last bag had frozen chicken breasts and a block of cheese.

It was Friday evening. Hunter had to make dinner. Plus he had to make three meals the next day. And three meals on Sunday.

"Hey, chef," Ethan said. "What's for dinner? I bet you are too chicken to cook."

Hunter ignored his little brother. He had an idea. The chicken and pasta could make a good meal. His mom made that a lot. But how did she do it? He had to think back.

The chicken was frozen. Hunter read the side of the bag. There were directions on how to thaw the meat. He could use the microwave for that. Then he could bake the chicken in the oven. Hunter preheated the oven while the chicken thawed. He decided to cook all the chicken that night.

Hunter read how to make the pasta. First he boiled water on the stove. Then he put the pasta in. He added a bit of salt too.

Hunter made a salad last. He chopped the lettuce and tomatoes. There was a salad bowl in the cupboard. Hunter got it out. Then he put the salad on the table.

Hunter liked having rolls for dinner. He took out one of the cans his mom bought. The oven was already preheated from the chicken. He put the rolls on a flat pan. Then he baked them.

"Dinner is served!" Hunter called out.

They all sat down to eat. His mom was happy. "Not bad," she said. "Good start."

"It was okay," Ethan replied. "Mom makes better chicken."

Saturday morning came. It was time for breakfast.

Hunter knew everyone liked eggs and toast. "How does Mom cook eggs?" he asked himself.

Hunter put some eggs in the microwave. He turned it on. *BANG. POP. BANG. POP.* The eggs exploded.

"Smart move," Ethan said. "Are you trying to kill us?"

"Stay out of my way," Hunter replied.

Hunter had to clean the microwave. It was a big mess.

"Mom uses a frying pan, you know," said Ethan.

Hunter rolled his eyes. But he took out a pan. Soon the eggs were cooking on the stove.

Then Hunter looked for a toaster. But he didn't see one. He looked at the oven. It had a broiler. He decided to use it to make toast.

Mom and Ethan ate the breakfast. "Not bad," Mom said.

"You burned my toast," Ethan said.

A few hours went by. It was time to make lunch.

"I want a big salad," their mom said. "How about that?"

Hunter had cooked all of the chicken breasts. He had put the extra ones in the refrigerator.

"Okay," Hunter replied.

Hunter took out the lettuce. He chopped some cooked chicken. Then he added some cheese and tomatoes. Lunch was made. Hunter served the chicken salad.

"Not bad," Mom said. "What's for dinner?"

"No more chicken!" Ethan said. "I want pizza!"

"Well, chef?" Mom asked. "How about it?"

Hunter thought about the groceries his mom bought. He had another idea.

It was nearly time for dinner. Hunter opened the second can of rolls. He rolled out the dough. This made a pizza crust. He baked the crust in the oven on a pizza pan.

Hunter topped the baked crust with chopped chicken. He added chopped tomatoes. Then he shredded cheese and sprinkled it on top.

"Wow!" Mom said. "Great job."

Ethan ate all of his pizza. Hunter grinned.

Hunter felt good. But he was scared. He was running out of food. And there were three more meals to make.

Sunday morning came. It was time for breakfast.

"I want French toast!" Ethan said.

"Can you do that?" Mom asked.

"Watch me," Hunter replied.

Hunter had to think. His mom made French toast all the time. How did she do it?

Hunter had a few eggs left. He needed to soak the bread in eggs. But that was not all.

"Milk!" Hunter said. He added milk to the eggs.

Hunter soaked the bread. He heated a pan on the stove. A pat of butter went into the pan. Then Hunter set the bread in the pan, slice by slice.

"Get the syrup," Hunter told Ethan.

"Did you really make French toast?" Ethan asked.

The family ate breakfast together. They laughed and talked.

"Not bad," their mom said. "You can make this for us anytime."

Hunter smiled. "I can make it better the next time."

"I am looking forward to lunch," she added.

"No chicken!" Ethan said. "Please, no more chicken."

Their mom laughed.

"How about a sandwich?" Hunter asked.

"You can't do that," Ethan replied. "That's not cooking. Mom said so."

Their mom smiled. "Hunter has done a great job. He can make sandwiches."

"Then I want peanut butter and jelly," Ethan replied.

"Mom did not buy that," Hunter said. "So you can't have it."

"It's okay," she replied. "There is some in the pantry. I will allow that. But only for Ethan."

It was soon time for lunch. Hunter looked at the food he had left. "I am going to win this bet," he said.

There were some tomatoes and lettuce. Half the loaf of bread was still there.

Only one chicken breast was left. Hunter decided to save it for dinner.

He knew how to make toast now. So he toasted the bread in the oven.

Hunter made Ethan a peanut butter and jelly sandwich. Then he had an idea. He cut the sandwich into the letter *E*.

Hunter gave Ethan his sandwich. "Look," Hunter said. "*E* for Ethan."

Ethan smiled.

Hunter made his mom a sandwich. He added mayo, sliced cheese, tomatoes, and lettuce. Then he sprinkled some salt and pepper on top.

"What did you make?" she asked.

"It's a toasted CLT," Hunter replied. "Cheese, lettuce, and tomato."

His mom bit into her sandwich. "Very good!"

"That's just a cheese sandwich," Ethan said.

Hunter rolled his eyes.

Sunday afternoon went by quickly. Dinner was soon.

Hunter was scared. He had one more meal to make. There was not much food left. The cheese was gone. Just a little chicken was left.

There was leftover pasta from Friday night. Some lettuce was left. So were a few slices of bread. There were plenty of tomatoes.

Hunter had an idea. He was going to make a sauce. First he grabbed the tomatoes. He turned on a burner. Then he cooked the tomatoes in a pan.

Hunter watched the tomatoes cook. They cooked on low heat for a long time. There were some spices in the cupboard. Hunter added a few. He took a taste. Then he added more spice.

His mom came into the kitchen. "Wow!" she said. "What are you making? That smells great."

"Don't look!" Hunter replied. "Go away! I don't want you to see it yet."

His mom smiled and walked away.

Dinner was almost ready. Hunter heated the last of the pasta. Then he chopped the last chicken breast.

The chicken went into the tomato sauce.

Hunter used the rest of the lettuce to make a salad. The last slices of bread went on the table.

They all sat down to eat.

"This is good," Ethan said.

Their mom smiled. "You did such a great job. I am very proud of you."

Hunter smiled. "Thanks."

Hunter was about to eat his last bite. "Mom," he said. "I have an idea."

"What's that?" she asked.

"I want to go to cooking school. I want to be a chef."

His mom smiled. "You will be a great chef."

Ethan rolled his eyes. "Oh no!"

"What's wrong?" Hunter asked.

"That will mean more chicken. No more chicken!"

JUST *flip* THE BOOK!

CARRIE GWYNNE

LIVING
SKILLS+

Cooking
Your Own
Meals

LIFESKILLS IN ACTION

It takes practice and planning to
be a great cook. Want to learn
more about how to cook smart?
Just flip the book!